スポーツのうた

Impressions of Sports

公益財団法人JAL財団＝編
Edited by JAL Foundation

ブロンズ新社
Bronze Publishing

歌舞伎と俳句

人間国宝・歌舞伎役者　中村吉右衛門

私の養父、初代中村吉右衛門は俳句を詠みました。高浜虚子先生の歳時記にも載せていただけるほどの句を詠んでいます。「秀山」という俳名も、それなりに世に知られています。

私は母方の祖父、初代吉右衛門に倅がなかったため、孫の私が養子となりました。歌舞伎の世界では、名を継ぐことを「襲名」といい、その名前の大きさ、また継ぐ役者の力量によって盛大さが違ってきます。初代は明治・大正・昭和にわたる名優の一人でした。それに肖れるよう、当時の私の力量以上の襲名披露をしていただきました。初代は芝居のための稽古事ばかりでなく、絵も書も学び、剣道や弓道も学びました。弓道は弓矢の正しい扱い、また姿勢を良くするためでもあります。絵画は美的センス、俳句は情操を深めるために学んだとのことです。

俳句にはもうひとつ、演技者として学ぶべきことがあります。まず写生、それから心に留まる心匠を削ぎおとし、搾りこむことだそうです。これは演技にもいえることで、無駄な動作や表情をせず、限られた内での外への呼びかけだからこそ、よりその役、その役者の心匠が伝わるようです。ですから、初代も俳句を懸命に勉強したのでしょう。

二代目の私はというと、子どものころ、初めて句作をしたのが

桜咲く　学校へ行く　子等たのし

——以来、句作はあきらめました。

なんとか役者としては吉右衛門の名を汚さぬよう、勤めてまいりました。そのひとつに、祥月の九月には「秀山祭」という初代を顕彰する公演を歌舞伎座でいたしております。

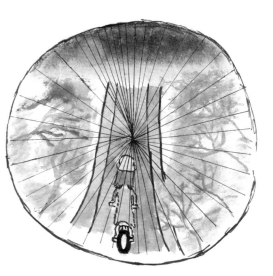

このたびのコロナ禍に際し

地球人　まけるな今こそ　手を結ぼう

Prologue

Kabuki and Haiku

Kichiemon Nakamura
Living National Treasure of Japan, Kabuki Actor

My adoptive father, the first Kichiemon Nakamura, wrote haiku. His haiku were good enough to be included in a saijiki (a season word almanac with example haiku) complied by Kyoshi Takahama, a grandmaster of haiku. His haiku name, "Shūzan," is known to the public accordingly.

The first Kichiemon was my grandfather on my mother's side. He did not have a son, so I was adopted. In the world of kabuki, inheriting a name is called "shūmei," and the grandeur depends on the value of the name and the ability of the actor who inherits it. The first Kichiemon was one of the greatest actors of the Meiji, Taishō, and Shōwa eras. To share his good fortune in passing on this prestigious name, he held a grand announcement of my "shūmei," even though his skill was beyond my ability at that time. The first Kichiemon had not only practiced lessons necessary for acting, but also learned painting, calligraphy, kendo, and Japanese archery. Archery served to teach the correct handling of bows and arrows, and to improve his posture. He is said to have learned painting to nurture his aesthetic sense and haiku to deepen his emotions.

There is one more lesson to learn from haiku as a performer. First, it is a sketch, and then it shaves off the ingenuity taking place in one's mind to narrow down to essence. This can be said of acting as well, where one acts without unnecessary movements or facial expressions, where a deliberately limited range seems to convey more of the performer's spirit and role. Therefore, the first Kichiemon must have learned haiku deeply.

As for me, the second Kichiemon, the first haiku I composed when I was a child was:

Cherry trees blooming
Children going to school
Are having fun

Since then, I have given up writing haiku.

As an actor, I have worked hard not to hurt the name and reputation of the first Kichiemon. To honor him, we are holding the Shūzan Festival at Kabuki Theater in September, the month when he passed away.

On the occasion of the novel coronavirus disaster:

We, the earthlings
Don't give up
Now is the time to join our hands

1章 たかく とおくへ
Higher and Farther

Step by step
Climbing up on colorful stones
Challenge myself

一步一步的
ㄅ ㄢ 爬在彩ㄙㄜˋ ㄕˊ ㄊ ㄡ ˋ 上
ㄊㄧㄠˇ ㄓ ㄢ ˋ 自已

歐 力誠
Aw Li-Chang
age 6　Taiwan（台湾／台北）

いっぽずつ
カラフルないしにのぼり
じぶんにいどむ

空を切って飛ぶ
心はドキドキ、あとには
粉雪の小道

Flying through the air
My heart is thumping, leaving
A trail of powder

Lucas Yang
age12
UK（英国）

限界に挑む
タカのように集中し
手足はゴムのように動く

Pushing the limits
Staying focused like a hawk
Limbs move like rubber

Gianna Kim
age10
Canada（カナダ）

Equestrian needs courage
Test of speed and endurance
Work well together!

马术需勇气
考验速度与耐力
配合真默契!

騎手には勇気がいる
スピードと持久力のテスト
一緒にがんばろう!

邹 慕优
Zou Muyou
age10
China（中国／上海）

马术
马术需勇气，
考验速度与耐力，
配合真默契！

四(2) 邹慕优 A2

小さな選手
水中では矢のように
勝つためにベストを尽くす

Cô vận động viên nhỏ
Như mũi tên lao nhanh dưới nước
Cố gắng giành chiến thắng

A small athlete
Like an arrow-head in the water
Try her best to win

Cô vận động viên nhỏ
Như mũi tên lao nhanh dưới nước
Cố gắng giành chiến thắng

Phan Nguyễn Gia Hân
Phan Nguyen Gia Han
age12
Vietnam（ベトナム）

オリンピック
僕（ぼく）は槍（やり）を投（な）げる
そしてオリンポスに届（とど）く

Olympics
I throw a javelin
And reach Olympus

Олимпиада…
Хвърлям копие
И достигам Олимп

Йозкан Беркант Еминов
Yozkan Berkant Eminov
age12
Bulgaria（ブルガリア）

サーフィンのレッスン
わたしは立ちあがれた
コーチがほめてくれた

Surf lesson
I can stand up
Professor praises me

Aula de surf
Consigo ficar de pé
Professor me elogia

Giovanna Monteiro Craveiro
age 8
Brazil（ブラジル）

用意、はじめ
はなれたり 突いたり
ぼくたちのフェンシング

On guard, ready, go
Move aside and attack
With our foils

En garde, prêt, allez
Esquirez et attaquez
Avec nos fleurets

Monarcha Arsène
age 9
France（フランス）

もうすぐオリンピック
私たちは応援！
さあ、盛りあがろう！

Olympics are near
And all we can do is cheer！
So let's celebrate！

Sofia Paolucci
age13
USA（米国／ボストン）

Olympics are near,
And all we can do is cheer!
So let's celebrate!

ぼくはスポーツをする
健康でいられる
笑顔のもとになる

Athletics I try
Helps me to be healthy fit
Gives reason to smile

Kavish Mehtani
age11
India（インド）

氷の上をすべる
すてきな思い出が戻ってくる
人生が楽しくなる

Skating on the ice
Sweet memories come alive
Brings joy to your life

Shayne Tang
age10
Singapore（シンガポール）

試合がはじまる
ボールが入った
わたしたちの勝ち

The match begins
The ball flies into the basket
We win the game

Matchen börjar nu
Bollen flyger i korgen
Vi vinner matchen

Ellen Palm
age10
Sweden（スウェーデン）

Two big wheels are moving
Two hands help unite body and mind
I would have run if I had legs

สองล้อใหญ่เคลื่อนที
สองมือหมุนร่วมแรงกายใจ
ถ้ามีขาคงวิ่ง

ธนัชชา คันธสาลี
Thanatcha Kantasalee
age11
Thailand（タイ）

ふたつの大きな車輪が動く
体と心をつなぐ二本の手
足があったら走っていたのに

ビーチコートで
あなたの肌がはねかえす音（おと）
日差（ひざ）しが強（つよ）くなる

From sea to beach
Your skin resounds
Sun rises as well

De mar a arena
Tu piel resuena y
El sol crecienta

Pérez Altamirano, Jimena Alejandra
age15
Mexico（メキシコ）

"De mar a arena
tu piel resuena y
el sol crecienta."
- Jimena Díaz

シュートして
流（なが）れるあせも
高（たか）くとぶ

Sinking a shot
My pouring sweat, too
Jumps high

高山 稀名
Malena Takayama
age11
Japan（日本）

ひと足（あし）ごと
本気（ほんき）で走（はし）る
集中（しゅうちゅう）して

Every step you take
Run with determination
Caught in the moment

Imbuido Ginelle
age14
USA（米国／グアム）

わたしのサッカーボール
緑（みどり）、白（しろ）、黒（くろ）でいい硬（かた）さ
さあ試合（しあい）よ

There lies my football
Green white black and nice hard
Ready to play

Daar ligt mijn voetbal
Groen wit zwart en lekker hard
Klaar om te spelen

Isa van der Sluis
age11
Netherlands（オランダ）

Bowling is so fun
Knocking down all of the pins
Wow! Another strike!

曾 建文
Marcus Tsang
age11
China（中国／香港）

ボウリングは楽しい
ピンを全部たおして
やった！またストライク！

The sound of the blade
Gliding through the ice
It greets me

Laurensia Josephine
age15
Indonesia（インドネシア）

スケートのエッジ
氷の上をシャーッとすべる
元気が出る

Ready, go!
Always feeling like
A cheetah

保井 一花
Ichika Yasui
age10
Japan（日本）

よーいドン
気持ちはいつも
チーターだ

日光が
車輪にあたり
私はまだ漕ぎつづける

Sunrays
In touch with bicycle wheels
I'm still biking

Saulės spinduliai
Liečia dviračio ratus
O aš vis minu

Aistė Mankauskaitė
Aiste Mankauskaite
age14
Lithuania（リトアニア）

Just like a shooting bullet
Breaking limitations
Run across the finish line

如子彈衝刺
發揮自我的極限
突破終點線

弾丸のように
限界を打ちやぶり
ゴールを走りぬける

尤 羿萱
You Yi-Hsuan
age14
Taiwan（台湾／台北）

風のように走る
進め、根気よく
オリンピック選手のように

Running like the wind
Pressing on, persevering
Like an olympian

Darius Lim Wei Chen
age13
Singapore（シンガポール）

なめらかな動き
氷の上の輝く白鳥
涙は隠して

In smooth motion
A glittering swan on the ice
The tears are hidden

Sujuvalt liikuv
Jääl lendlev sädelev luik
Pisarad peidus

Liisi Kõrvits
age12
Estonia（エストニア）

ボールが転がる
選手が見ている
汗がしたたる

The ball rolls
The player observes
Sweat falls

El balón rueda
El jugador observa
El sudor cae

Luis Felipe Dávila Paredes
age13
Ecuador（エクアドル）

ボールを打ちくだく
ベースをまわって
先へ先へと

I destroy the ball
Run around the basses
Going going gone

Thomas Suzuki
age 9
USA（米国／ハワイ）

Still failing to beat back
Throwing shuttlecock up
Racket in hand

Nespėju mušti
Metu muselę viršun
Raketė rankoj

Milda Antanaitytė
Milda Antanaityte
age12
Lithuania（リトアニア）

なかなか相手をたおせない
バドミントンの羽根を投げて
手にはラケット

Flushing all over the face
Like a reinless wild horse
Bravely charge forward

滿臉紅通通
如脫繮的野馬般
勇敢向前衝

李 昱君
Lee Yu-Chun
age12
Taiwan（台湾／台北）

顔が真っ赤
野馬のように
勇敢に前へ走る

16

We go swimming
There are bubbles in the water
They disappear

泳ぎにいく
水中の泡が
消えてゆく

Menemme uimaan
Vedessä on kuplia
Ne katoavat

Karjalainen Pinja
age10
Finland（フィンランド）

17

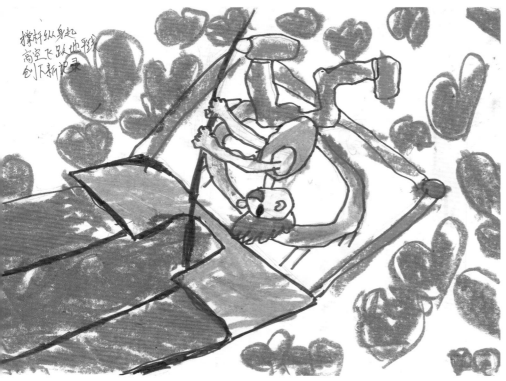

ぼうたかとびでジャンプして
ちへいせんをこえてそらたかく
しんきろくだ

I jump up with a pole vault
Flying over the horison
Set a new record

撑杆纵身起
高空飞跃地平线
创下新纪录

周 冠宸
Zhou Guanchen
age 6
China（中国／天津）

バッターが構え(かま)
ピッチャーが振り(ふ)かぶる
3、2、1、ホームラン！

The batter is ready
The pitcher is winding up
Three, two, one, Homerun!

Penny Lane McPeak
age 9
USA（米国／ニューヨーク）

情熱(じょうねつ)を持(も)って
スポーツする
オリンピックを目指(めざ)して

With passion
We do sports
Olympic life

Dengan semangat
Kita bermain sukan
Hidup Olimpik

Lee Yuk Yan
age11
Malaysia（マレーシア）

シャトルラン
走(はし)って走(はし)って
新記録(しんきろく)

Shattle run
I run and run
Toward a new record!

三輪 眞己
Masaki Miwa
age 9
Japan（日本）

十段の
未知なるかべへ
走り出す

A 10-box vaulting box
Toward its unknown wall
I start running

寺島 凌吾
Ryogo Terashima
age12
Japan（日本）

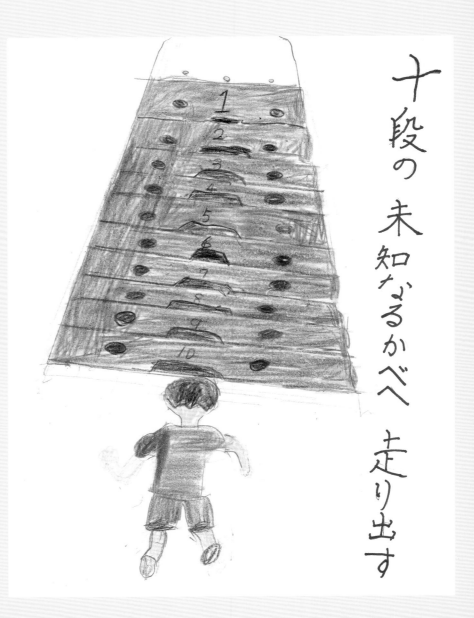

十段の 未知なるかべへ 走り出す

やさしく とてもやさしく
こおりもたのしんでる
わたしのスケートを

Soft very soft
The ice enjoys
Of my skating

Suave muy suave
El hielo disfruta
De mi patinaje

Lucciana Valeska Ríos Bayas
age 6
Ecuador（エクアドル）

フェンシングの剣を手に
身をかわし、相手をブロックし、突く
笑って、堂々と

Fencing in hand
Dodge, Block, Thorn
Laugh and be proud

手握软青锋
闪转腾挪格挡刺
笑傲群芳立

刘 尹若
Liu Yinruo
age 8
China（中国／上海）

Suave muy suave
el hielo disfruta
de mi patinaje

手を伸ばし
あと一センチと
水をかく

Stretching my hand
For another centimeter
I swim through the water

中井 心春
Koharu Nakai
age12
Japan（日本）

手を伸ばし
あと一センチと
水をかく

Thunder smash
National victory
Support from the people

Pukulan kilat
Kemenangan negara
Sokongan rakyat

雷のようなスマッシュ
マレーシアの勝利
みんなからの応援で

Poo Zhang Jen
age10
Malaysia（マレーシア）

Without fear of failure
If you challenge
You already win

不要怕失败
只要你肯去挑战
你已经赢了

失敗をおそれず
挑戦さえすれば
もう君の勝ち

王 炳梵
Wang Bingfan
age 8
China（中国／天津）

22

ぬれた額
雨のように
光の矢

Wet forehead
Thoughts like rain
Arrows of light

Fronte bagnata
Pensieri come pioggia
Frecce di luce

Rudi Ghersetti
age15
Italy（イタリア）

太陽（たいよう）があたためる
上（あ）がる水（みず）しぶき
飛（と）びこむと

Warms the sun
Dripping water
When they fly

Aquece o sol
Os pingos da água
Quando eles voam

Daniela Sequeira de Sousa
age15
Portugal （ポルトガル）

Aquece o sol
os pingos da água
quando eles voam

Grandma likes petanque
She throws the boules precisely
Her grandchildren take her out for show

คุณยายชอบเปตอง
โยนลูกเหล็กได้อย่างแม่นย่า
ลูกหลานพาออกงาน

นิลพัทธ์ ชินปา
Ninlaphat Chinpa
age11
Thailand （タイ）

おばあちゃんはペタンクが好（す）き
ブールを正確（せいかく）に投（な）げる
孫（まご）たちがショーに連（つ）れていく

Balanced at the top
Gazing at the sea of white
Weightless, as I glide

Marcus Soothill
age14
Canada （カナダ）

てっぺんでバランス
白（しろ）い海（うみ）を見（み）つめて
すべりだせば無重力（むじゅうりょく）

The delicate leap
Floating dress,
The graceful dance.

しなやかなジャンプ
ふわっとしたドレス
優雅なダンス

The delicate leap
Floating dress
The graceful dance

Saltul delicat
Rochie plutind
În graţiosul dans

Ilinca Martiniana
age14
Romania（ルーマニア）

Making up my mind
Fly to blue sky with dreams
Drawing a skyline

揮出的決意
乗著夢飛向青天
畫出天際線

決心する
夢に乗って青空へ
放物線を描け

秦 桐彤
Chin Tun-Tun
age14
Taiwan（台湾／台北）

Morning exercise
Everyone sends his ball
Up towards the sun

Jutarnja vježba
Svatko šalje svoju loptu
Prema suncu

朝の練習
みんながボールを投げる
太陽に向かって

Dinko Galik
Dinko Galik
age12
Croatia（クロアチア）

25

青春の車輪
風を追う少年
夢はいつもその先に

Youth flying wheel
A boy in pursuit of the wind
Dreams is always ahead

青春飛転着車輪
追風的少年
梦想永遠在前方

李 冠廷
Li Guanting
age15
China（中国／大連）

走る息子を見守る
転んで立ってまた走る
お父さんの誇らしげな笑顔

Seeing his son running
Falling then standing up and running again
Dad smiles with pride

มองลูกเล่นกีฬา
ลูกล้มแล้วลุกขึ้นวิ่งต่อ
พ่อยิ้มอย่างภูมิใจ

ภัทรา เฉลียวไว
Phatra Chaleawwai
age12
Thailand（タイ）

目ざめた心
体で表現
精神統一

Awakened mind
The body expresses itself
Completed soul

Mente despierta
El cuerpo se expresa
Alma completa

Danica Chacín Didencu
age14
Ecuador（エクアドル）

胸の鼓動
クールな輝き
青い光

The heart beat
Cool sparkle
Blue light

Debaran jantung
Percikan sejuk nyaman
Cahaya biru

Aw Chui Ying
age13
Malaysia（マレーシア）

あわだてて
みずをかきわけ
ゴールまで

Forming bubbles
Swimming through the water
To reach the goal

福家 要
Kaname Fuke
age 5
Japan（日本）

最高の気分
この手を伸ばして
ボールをレシーブ

Get satisfied
My arms go to
Receive the ball

La satisfacción
En los brazos al hacer
Una recepción

Takahashi Slim, Aiko
age15
Mexico（メキシコ）

ボールが飛んで
ファンが息をのむ
幸せいっぱい

Ball flight
Fan's breath stopped
Euphoria

Lot piłki
Oddech fana wstrzymany
Euforia

Natalia Pikula
Natalie Pikula
age10
Poland（ポーランド）

人生はレース
追いかける夢と目標がある
自分のためにがんばる

Life is like a race
I have goals with dreams to chase
Strive to earn my place

Lacson Micah
age13
USA（米国／グアム）

馬術競技
ジャンプのときは
目をとじる

Equestrian event
At the time of the jump
I close my eyes

Prova de hipismo
No momento do salto
Fecho meus olhos

Maria Letícia Slompo
age 9
Brazil（ブラジル）

馬は速く走る
疲れを知らず
勇気を出して走る

A horse runs fast
Not knowing fatigue
Runs with courage

马儿跑的快
不怕晒也不怕累
勇往向前衝

罗 雪菲
Luo Xuefei
age10
China（中国／広州）

馬儿跑的快
不小白晒也不忙
勇往向前衝

スイミングプール
まっすぐ泳いで、いいタイム
無我夢中(むがむちゅう)

In the swimming pool
Keep in straight line, making quick time
Can't see a thing

Sean Maher
age13
Ireland（アイルランド）

みんなの応援(おうえん)
私(わたし)はまだレース中(ちゅう)
負(ま)けと分(わ)かっていても

Cheering all around
I still keep racing
Knowing I will lose, though

เสียงเชียร์ดังไปทั่ว
ฉันยังคงแข่งขันต่อไป
ถึงรู้ว่าต้องแพ้

ปัญชิกา ปัทมกุลเศรษฐ์
Panchika Patamakulset
age15
Thailand（タイ）

燃(も)える赤(あか)
雷(かみなり)のキック
攻撃(こうげき)準備(じゅんび)完了(かんりょう)

Blazing red
Thunderous kick
Ready to attack

Merah Membara
Tendangan Halilintar
Siap Menerjang

Bagas Satrio
age13
Indonesia（インドネシア）

As I dance I move
Silently across the floor
Feeling the music

踊りながら
静かにフロアを横切る
音楽に合わせて

Annica Mody
age11
USA（米国／サンディエゴ）

Beginning
Thrill, expectation
Music

Начало
Тръпка, очакване
Музика

はじまる
スリルと期待
音楽

Василия Христо Елезова
Vassilia Christo Elezova
age12
Bulgaria（ブルガリア）

Don't take force
To play the game
Wisdom is needed

बलले हैन
खेल खेल्नको लागि
बुद्धि चाहिन्छ

がんばるだけじゃダメだ
考えて
競うんだ

रोहण कार्की
Rohan Khatri
age10
Nepal（ネパール）

Eco de aplausos
en la cancha de baloncesto.
la lluvia en el exterior...

会場いっぱいに拍手
バスケットボールのコートに
外は雨

Applause echo
On the basketball court
Raining outside

Eco de aplausos
En la cancha de baloncesto
La lluvia en el exterior...

Margarita Espín Sola
age12
Spain （スペイン）

わたしは登る…高く
みんながわたしを見ている
勇気を出して、飛べるかな？

I am rising . . . high
Everyone's eyes on me
With courage, will I fly?

Marta Ciszek
Martha Ciszek
age 8
Poland （ポーランド）

的を見つめて
的の真んなかをねらって
金へ向かって

Eyes on the target
Towards the bull's eye it goes
Going for the gold

Yeo Ka Ing
age11
Singapore （シンガポール）

夢に見た場所
そして今 私はここにいる
夢をかなえるために

Mi sueño era este
y ahora estoy aquí
para cumplirlo.

My dream was here
And I'm here to
Make my dream come true

Mi sueño era este
Y ahora estoy aquí
Para cumplirlo

González Alaluf, Natalia Constanza
age14 Mexico（メキシコ）

osmijeh sirena
usklađeni pokreti
vrtlog glazbe

人魚のほほえみ
ひとつに動く
音楽の渦

Mermaid smiles
Movements as one
The whirl of music

Osmijeh sirena
Usklađeni pokreti
Vrtlog glazbe

Ema Tadić
Ema Tadic
age 8
Croatia（クロアチア）

34

爷爷教太极，
莫笑一人一个样，
春色映笑脸。

おじいちゃんは太極拳を教える
すこしくらいちがっても笑わない
春のような笑顔

Granpa teaches tai chi
Never laughs at small differences
Spring smile

爷爷教太极
莫笑一人一个样
春色映笑脸

王 冠琳
Wang Guanlin
age11
China（中国／天津）

家族旅行
海の高い波に
サーファーたち

Vacation tour
In the high waves of the sea
A group of surfers

Passeio de férias
Nas altas ondas do mar
Grupo de surfistas

Alina Vitória Kaneske Gomes
age 9
Brazil（ブラジル）

夢を抱いて
よく生きて、いっぱい愛して
いっぱい笑って

Hang on to your dreams
Live well, love lots
And laugh often

蔣 善熒
Chiang Sin Ying Hester
age 9
China（中国／香港）

試合はいつだって
勝ち負けじゃない
プレーを楽しもう

A game is not always
About whether you win or you lose
Play to learn, have fun

Khushal Sharma
age12
India（インド）

チョンカのボード
ビー玉を穴に入れていく
すごく楽しい

My congkak board
Fill up with marble
So much fun

Papan congkakku
Isi guli deretan
Menyeronokan

Cheah Pui San, Nicole
age14
Malaysia（マレーシア）

一緒に
楽しむ
バスケットボール

We together
Playing basketball
Rejoice

हामी मिलेर
बास्केटबल खेल्दै
खुसी मनायौं

मुबिना गिरी
Mubina Giri
age11
Nepal（ネパール）

You kick a ball, sometimes you fall
And at times you stand tall
This is the magic of football

Shrayan Pradhan
age11
Bhutan（ブータン）

ボールをけって、ときどき転んで
また、しっかり立ちあがって
それがサッカーの不思議

水のなかで
素早かったり遅かったり
どこも泳ぐ人だらけ

Water by water
Quick and slow swimmers everywhere
Some fast and some slow

Ann Rebecca Alfred
age 8
USA（米国／ダラス）

泳ぐことは命
青い海
君と泳ぐ

Swimming life
Blue oceans
I swim with you

Natación vida
Océanos azules
Nado contigo

Nicolás Alejandro Vega Avilés
age 8
Ecuador（エクアドル）

エトワールダンサー
星のまわりを踊り
月面でスピン

A dancer of etoile
Dance around the stars
The spin on the moon

Une danseuse étoile
Danse autour des étoiles
Puis virvolte sur la lune

Ruot Victor
age 8
France（フランス）

Let's do sports
Strengthening relationship
The body is healthy

Mari bersukan
Mengeratkan hubungan
Badan pun sihat

スポーツで
絆を強く
体も健康に

Muhammad Ariff Zafran Bin Azman
age12
Malaysia（マレーシア）

Boxing as if getting real angry
Here comes a sudden ring
Taking off boxing gloves, I embrace my pal

เตะต่อยเหมือนโกรธกัน
เสียงระฆังดังขึ้นทันใด
ถอดนวมกอดคอเพื่อน

นวรัตน์ กมลคุณอัครสิริ
Navarat Kamolkoonakkarasiri
age12
Thailand（タイ）

怒っているみたいにボクシング
突然のゴング
グローブを外して相手と抱きあう

Blood and sweat
Mud splashes on goggles
The end is near

Veri ja higi
Pori pritsmed prillidel
Lõpp on lähedal

Romet Pajur
age15
Estonia（エストニア）

汗と血と
泥がゴーグルにはねて
ゴールはもうすぐ

地面にスパイク
高いネットを越えて
あなたの腕からパス

Pass it with your arms
Set it over the tall net
Spike me to the ground

Villareal Arielle Marie
age11
USA（米国／グアム）

育てたい
友情と平和の心を
シーソー遊び

Seesaw game
Of friendship and peace
Our desire

ढिकीच्याउ खेल
मित्रता र शान्तिको
हाम्रो चाहना

अनिता श्रेष्ठ
Anita Shrestha
age13
Nepal（ネパール）

スポーツの魂だ
根性もきたえて
体をきたえて

Maintain your fitness
Strengthen your mindset
The spirit of sport

鍛鍊好體能
堅毅恆心同兼備
體育真精神

趙 梓舜
Chiu Tsz Shun Jake
age10
China（中国／香港）

Swimming is fun
We can swim and play
Swimming is fun for everyone

Aina Saito
age 7
USA（米国／サンフランシスコ）

水泳はおもしろいな
泳いで遊んで
水泳はみんなで楽しめる

Swimming is fun
We can swim and play
Swimming is fun for everyone

Sports teaches sacrifice
For the team because
Winning is our dream

スポーツは我慢することを教える
チームのために だって
勝つことが夢だから

Sanskriti Kishor Tichkar
age13
India（インド）

Severe tug-of-war competition
Pulling the rope cooperatively
Insist on winning

拔河生死戰
通力合作拉繩索
堅持得勝利

綱引きの激戦
力を合わせて綱を引く
勝つんだ

莊 昀臻
Chuang Yun-Chen
age11
Taiwan（台湾／高雄）

In the home garden
I play volleyball with my friend
Happy moment

No jardim de casa
Jogo vôlei com a amiga
Momento feliz

家の庭で
友だちとバレーボール
楽しいひととき

Giovana da Silveira de Freitas
age11
Brazil（ブラジル）

43

Let's jump rope
It's great for weightloss and increase height
Let's enjoy

快來跳繩吧
減肥增高好處多
愉快樂其中

梁 詩珩
Leung Sze Hang
age10
China（中国／香港）

縄とびしよう
背が伸びるし 体も軽くなるし
みんなで楽しもう

Teamwork is a must
When playing sports it is fun
So enjoy, have trust

Gomez Alexandra
age13
USA（米国／グアム）

チームワークが大事
スポーツはおもしろい
だから楽しんで、チームを信頼して

Together we fly kite
More happier we became when
moment drives pain away.

一緒に凧上げ
上がったときはうれしくて
つらい思いも飛んでいく

Together we fly kite
More happier we become
When moment drives pain away

सँगै चङ्गा उडाउँदा
अझ बढी खुसी भयौं
जुन क्षण पिडा टाढा भयौ

आकृति राई
Aakriti Rai
age15
Nepal（ネパール）

バレーボール
ビーチでしなやか
高い波(たかいなみ)

Volleyball
Agile on the beach
Rough sea

La pallavolo
Agili sulla spiaggia
Mare agitato

Tiziana Balint
age15
Italy（イタリア）

La pallavolo
agili sulla spiaggia
mare agitato

競争(きょうそう)よりも調和(ちょうわ)
しかし
友情(ゆうじょう)が一番(いちばん)

Harmony is stronger than competition
But
Friendship is priceless

P.D.Chenitha Mansilu
age13
Sri Lanka（スリランカ）

プールで泳(およ)ぐ
楽(たの)しい魚(さかな)のように
自由自在(じゆうじざい)

Swimming in the pool
Happy as a little fish
It's free and easy

游泳池裡游
像快樂的小魚兒
自由又自在

游 子弘
You Zi-Hong
age 8
Taiwan（台湾／高雄）

集中して
みんな歩いたり走ったり
ひとりのランナーが優勝

They are concentrated
All trot and run
A runner wins

Ils sont concentrés
Tous trottinent et s'élancent
Un coureur gagne

Bagayoko Madina
age10
France（フランス）

さあこれから試合
7時にはじまって
わたしたちが勝った わーい

Now we will play
The game starting at 7
We won the game yea

Nu ska vi spela
Matchen börjar klockan 7
Vi vann matchen Ja

Ida Byström
age10
Sweden（スウェーデン）

Ils sont concentrés
Tous trottinent et s'élancent
Un coureur gagne

女の子もスポーツ
野球、サッカー、どれも楽しい
一緒にやろうね

Girls can do sports too
Baseball, soccer, are all fun
Let's play together

Ellie Minami
age10
USA（米国／サンフランシスコ）

学校でトーナメント
大勢の友だちと
卓球だ

School tournament
The crowd of friends
At table tennis

Torneio da escola
A torcida dos amigos
No tênis de mesa

Nadielly Carolini de Lima Francisco
age 9
Brazil（ブラジル）

あたたかな日差し
校庭で遊びまわる
楽しい休み時間

In the warm sunshine
Runing and jumping on the campus
Merrily get out of school

溫暖的陽光
校園內跑跑跳跳
開心的下課

徐 珮喬
Syu Pei-Chiao
age 8
Taiwan（台湾／台北）

ワクワクする夕方
石けり遊びで深まる
すてきな友情

Exciting evening
Of stappoo gives us love
Friendship with fun

Pragya Kar
age11
India（インド）

人々の虹
高く上がった旗
それらを振って

A rainbow of people
Flags raised high
Waving them on

Alyssa Martinez
age13
UK（英国）

あせの玉
まわりを見れば
てきばかり

Beads of sweat
As I look around
Enemies everywhere

長尾 玲奈
Reina Nagao
age 7
Japan（日本）

Red and big sun
Like a ball follows the soccers
Awaiting for summer in Japan

Mặt trời tròn đỏ rực
Như quả bóng theo chân cầu thủ
Đang đợi hè nước Nhật

赤く大きな太陽
サッカーボールのような
日本の夏を楽しみに

Hà Xuân Thảo Trâm
Ha Xuan Thao Tram
age14
Vietnam（ベトナム）

Running deers
Wore on their antlers
Crown of laurel

Koşan geyikler
Takmış boynuzlarına
Defneden tacı

走る鹿たち
ツノにつけてる
月桂樹のかんむり

Damla Nira Aksöz
Damla Nira Aksoz
age11
Turkey（トルコ）

水を感じる
腕と足に
喜びでいっぱい

Feel the water
By my arms and legs
My heart is filled with happiness

Al sentir el agua
Entre mis brasos y mis piernas
Mi corazón se llena de alegria

González Vargas, Alexa
age 9
Mexico（メキシコ）

Al sentir
agua entr
mis bras
mis piern
mi cora
se llena
alegria.

Dancing ballet
Gracefully and charmingly
Shine on the stage

跳個芭蕾舞
輕步曼舞姿如媚
閃爍在舞台上

バレエを踊る
足どり軽く　姿美しく
舞台で輝く

王 宜亭
Wang Yi-Ting
age10
Taiwan（台湾／台北）

Player dolphin
Competed with boats
Till seagull chirped

Oyuncu yunus
Yarıştı teknelerle
Martı ötene dek

Doğa Merze
Doga Merze
age13
Turkey（トルコ）

選手はイルカ
競いあった　船たちと
カモメが鳴くまで

Ba spelar fotboll
Med sin kompis Annika
Dom spelar mot Åsa

イサはサッカーをする
友<small>とも</small>だちのアニカと一緒<small>いっしょ</small>に
アーサが相手<small>あいて</small>

Isa plays football
With her friend Annika
Playing against Asa

Isa spelar fotboll
Med sin kompis Annika
Dom spelar mot Åsa

Tilde Fredin
age10
Sweden（スウェーデン）

運動場<small>うんどうじょう</small>
勝<small>か</small>つか負<small>ま</small>けるか
この場所<small>ばしょ</small>で

Playground
Bring that to you
Win or lose

खेल मैदान
ल्यायौ की तिमीले
जित या हार

सिद्धार्थ सापकोटा
Siddhartha Sapkota
age14
Nepal（ネパール）

冬<small>ふゆ</small>から春<small>はる</small>へ
天使<small>てんし</small>たちはウイルスとたたかう
オリンピックは来年<small>らいねん</small>に

From winter to spring
Angels fight virus
Olympic Games wait for next year

冬去春来半
天使逆行歼病毒
奥运等明年

单 思缘
Shan Siyuan
age13
China（中国／天津）

52

雨のなかで踊って
高くジャンプ
気分もさわやか

Dancing in the rain
I jump up high in the air
It is relieving

Tanzen im Regen
Ich springe hoch in die Luft
Es ist befreiend

Anastasia Fink
age11
Germany（ドイツ）

Tanzen im Regen
Ich springe hoch in die Luft
Es ist befreiend

Skipping as a kangaroo jumping
It's fun to jump up and down
Making us healthy and happy

ㄊㄧㄠˋ ㄕㄥˊ ㄒㄧㄤˋ ㄉㄞˋ ㄕㄨˇ
ㄊㄧㄠˋ 高ㄊㄧㄠˋ 低ㄓㄣ 好玩
ㄐㄧㄢˋ ㄎㄤㄧㄡˋ 快樂

洪 睿婕
Hong Jui-Chieh
age 7
Taiwan（台湾／高雄）

カンガルーみたいに縄とび
上へ下へピョンピョンと
健康で楽しい

Some times I win
Some times I lose
Win or lose I love sports

Thanumi De Silva
age 5
Sri Lanka（スリランカ）

かつときもある
まけるときもある
かってもまけてもスポーツがすき

3章 たいようのしたで
Under The Sun

赤い円盤が
地平線にあらわれて
朝のゴールイン！

Red disk
Flows to the horizon
The finish of morning!

Raudonas diskas
Už horizonto skrieja
Ryto finišas!

Dominyka Švėgždaitė
Dominyka Svegzdaite
age13　Lithuania（リトアニア）

鳥のように飛ぶ
美しい地球を見ながら
上から見ると私はとても小さい

Fly like a bird
Seeing the beauty of the earth
From above I feel very small

Terbang seperti burung
Melihat indahnya bumi
Dari atas ku merasa sangat kecil

Sydney Carina Halim
age11
Indonesia（インドネシア）

てとあしと
こころがさきに
おどりだす

My hands, feet
And my heart
Start dancing first

久冨 蔀乃
Fukino Hisatomi
age 8
Japan（日本）

光輝く堤防
星に導かれて
さいごまで泳ぐ

Shiny banks embrace
The guiding star leads
Swim to the end

Žvilgančiuos krantuos
Palei kelrodę žvaigždę
Plaukiu pabaigon

Neringa Radajevaitė
Neringa Radajevaite
age12
Lithuania（リトアニア）

ザブンと飛びこみ
美しく水をかく
魚のように自由

Jumping into a pool with a splash
Swims a beautiful arc by hand
Free as a fish

噗通！入水中
划出美麗的弧線
如魚兒自在

林 亮宇
Lin Liang-Yu
age 9
Taiwan（台湾／高雄）

噗通！入水中
划出美麗的弧線
如魚兒自在

I will ride a horse
Ride into the forest
Jumping with my horse

Jag ska rida häst
Jag ska rida i skogen
Jag hoppar med häst

Leia Nordin Sand
age10
Sweden（スウェーデン）

馬に乗る
森へ向かって
馬と一緒にジャンプ

The rays of the moon
Throws away the fishing rod
For a fisherman

Razele soarelui
Aruncă undiţa
Pentru pescar

Criciu Cristian
age12
Romania（ルーマニア）

月が光の
釣糸を垂らす
漁師のために

風にゆれる
波に乗る帆
夕日とともに

Dance with wind
Sails in the waves
With the sunset

Danço ao vento
Uma vela nas ondas
Com o pôr-do-sol

Maria Carolina Rodrigues Lopes
age15
Portugal（ポルトガル）

White waves in the sea
A surfboard glide on it
Makes the hot summer day cooler

Sóng tung bọt trắng xóa
Tấm ván lướt nhẹ trên mặt biển
Làm mát cả trưa hè

海には白い波
サーフボードが海面をすべる
暑い夏の日も涼しくなる

Bùi Đặng Khánh Như
Bui Dang Khanh Nhu
age12
Vietnam（ベトナム）

Summer
On the edge of the wave
White meerschaum dances

夏
波の端に
白い泡が踊る

Лято
По острието на вълната
Танцува бяла пяна

Асена Ахмедова Арифова
Asena Ahmedova Arifova
age13
Bulgaria（ブルガリア）

Rustle of leaves
Running down the path
Wind in the face

Crujir de hojas
Corriendo por la senda
Viento en la cara

落ち葉をガサゴソ
道を走っていると
顔に風

Lucía Martínez Honrubia
age14
Spain（スペイン）

Crujir de hojas,
corriendo por la senda
viento en la cara

Diploma on the wall
A spider slides over
Outgrown skates

Diploma na zidu
Pauk proklizava
Prerasle klizaljke

壁の賞状の上を
クモがすべっていく
小さくなったスケート靴

Mia Vlahović
Mia Vlahovic
age12
Croatia（クロアチア）

Don't use force
Walking through
Snow far away

Nie używaj siły
Idąc przez
Śnieg daleki

力を使わず
雪のなか
遠くまで歩く

Antoni Gaj
Anthony Gaj
age10
Poland（ポーランド）

A dream comes true
For a while you become
A bird

Сбъдната мечта
За миг ставаш
Птица

Елена Светланова Деянова
Elena Svetlanova Deyanova
age15
Bulgaria （ブルガリア）

夢がかなう
すこしのあいだ
鳥になる

My colourful sailboat
Dances with waves
Towards the finish

Renkli yelkenlim
Dans eder dalgalarla
Bitişe doğru

Seher İlter
Seher Ilter
age 7
Turkey （トルコ）

カラフルなわたしのヨット
波たちと踊るよ
ゴールに向かって

Hajime the beginning
Sun beams on the playmat
Look shimmering dust

Hajime begin
Zonnestralen op de mat
Kijk glinsterstof

Philip Mol
age 5
Netherlands （オランダ）

やあ！さいしょに
あさひが げんかんマットに
ほら、ちりがゆれてる

60

風のように走る
日差しのなかを素早く
このスポーツこそ最高

I run like the wind
Swiftly gliding in the sun
This sport is great fun

Isabella Bredt
age10
USA（米国／サンディエゴ）

Swift as the wind

By: Isabella B

I run like the wind.
Swiftly gliding in the sun.
This sport is great fun.

水がはねる
赤い葉がプールに落ちる
水は冷たい

The water splashes
A red leaf falls in the pool
The water is cold

Vitaline-Ivanka Akimeida Diaz-Petrova
age12
USA（米国／ボストン）

The water splashes
A red leaf falls in the pool
The water is cold

夏
色の渦のなかを
夢に向かって高く飛ぶ

Summer
In the swirl of colours
I fly high to the dreams

Лято
Във вихъра на цветовете
Политам към мечтите

Петя Добромирова Димитрова
Petya Dobromirova Dimitrova
age 9
Bulgaria（ブルガリア）

太陽は強く照りつける
さあプールへいこう
背も伸びる

The sun shines so hard
Let's go to the swimming pool
To make ourselves tall

Nắng hè oi ả quá
Hãy cùng nhau đến hồ bơi nào
Nhất định sẽ thêm cao

Lê Ngọc Cát Tường
Le Ngoc Cat Tuong
age12
Vietnam（ベトナム）

女子のスケート
地球の上で競争
誰が一着？

Girls' skate
Racing on the earth
Who will come first?

女子滑冰赛
在地球上拼一拼
谁是第一呀

徐 佳慧
Xu Jiahui
age 8
China（中国／天津）

A shiny red ball
Bouncing around the green pitch
Summer has arrived

輝く真っ赤なボール
緑のピッチではずむ
夏が来た

Aarna Gandhi
age 9
UK（英国）

The bike
Jumps into the sun
Like a hawk

自転車が
太陽へ飛びこむ
タカのように

La bicicletta
Salta verso il sole
Come un falco

Federico Castellan
age 9
Italy（イタリア）

自転車を力いっぱいこぐ
台湾の景色をぐんぐん通りすぎ
風に向かって走るぼくはとてもかっこいい

Striving to ride a bicycle
Taiwan's scenery whistling past
Facing the wind the most cool man I am

鐵馬奮力踩
寶島風光呼嘯閃
迎風我最帥

鄭 旭廷
Cheng Hsu-Ting
age11
Taiwan（台湾／高雄）

ぼくのはだか馬と
風のなかを走る
ユーカリの匂いがする

With my unsaddled horse
Running in the wind
Feeling the smell of eucalyptus

Con mi caballo a pelo
Corriendo en el viento
Sintiendo el olor de eucalipto

Carlos Mitsuho Novoa Okubo
age11
Ecuador（エクアドル）

Con mi caballo a pelo
Corriendo en el viento
Sintiendo el olor de eucalipto

64

I wear my goggles
I jump into the big pool
I love the water

Evageline Hong Hui En
age 7
Singapore（シンガポール）

ゴーグルをつけて
大きなプールに飛びこむ
水が大好き

65

I'm a little expert swimmer
Like a fish in water
The crab is watching me

游泳小能手
如鱼得水水中游
螃蟹一旁瞅

季 昕祎
Ji Xinyi
age 9
China（中国／上海）

わたしは小さな水泳選手
水のなかでは魚のよう
カニがわたしを見てる

Keeping a rhythm along
The peaceful silence blooms like
Birds dancing lightly

Alin Chen
age12
USA（米国／ボストン）

リズムをきざめば
静けさが花開く
軽やかに踊る鳥みたいに

雪の上のソリ遊び
ひっくり返るのは楽しい
雪まみれ

Sleighing on the snow
It's fun to tumble upside down
Snowy all over

Kelguga tore
On kummuli kukkuda
Kõik saab lumiseks

Marie Pilvistu
age 8
Estonia（エストニア）

矢を放つ
顔にはまぶしい太陽
ドキッとした

I shoot an arrow
The bright sun shines in my face
My heart skips a beat

Ashley Shen
age10
Canada（カナダ）

The sun on my face
As I fly through the blurred world
Hooves and hearts in sync

Hannah Rayner
age13
UK（英国）

顔に日を受け
まぶしい世界を進めば
ひづめと心はひとつ

A girl runs
She doesn't step on the flower
She comes home

La niña corre
No pisa las flores
Llega a casa

María García Ibáñez
age 5
Spain（スペイン）

おんなのこがはしる
はなをふまないように
いえにかえる

落下する
私は鳥、風、空になる
ロープにつながれたまま

I fall through the air
I'm a bird, the wind, the sky
Anchored by a cord

Sophia Killawee
age13
Canada（カナダ）

I fall through the air
I'm a bird, the wind, the sky
Anchored by a cord

Dancing a moonlight dance
Dancing in the cold snow light
The cold moonlight

Dansar i månskensdans
Dansar i snöns kalla sken
Månens kalla sken

Tova Dalethsson
age10
Sweden（スウェーデン）

月光のダンスを踊る
冷たい雪あかりのなかで踊る
冷たい月の光

A bicycle in the shed
With forest trails waiting ahead
In a snowed-in yard

Kuuris on ratas
Ees ootab metsarada
Õues ikka hanged

Karola Eliise Hütter
age10
Estonia（エストニア）

物置の自転車を
森の道が待っている
雪に埋もれた庭で

68

一呼吸
冬をすいこみ
地面ける

One deep breath
Breathing in the winter
I kick the ground

荒野 百花
Momoka Arano
age13
Japan（日本）

As many times
As the number of sunflower seeds
I swing my bat

村山 惺南
Sena Murayama
age 9
Japan（日本）

ひまわりの
たねのかずほど
バットふる

A spring in my step
Pirouette like pink petals
Falling from a tree

Maya Williamson
age11
UK（英国）

弾むステップ
ピルエットは
木から舞いちるピンクの花びら

Leaves cover
The baseball field
The ball is hidden

Las hojas cubren
El campo de béisbol
Se esconde la bola

Eva Moreno Gallego
age13
Spain（スペイン）

落ち葉におおわれた
野球場
ボールが見えなくなった

70

長く真っ白な雪のゲレンデ
日の出とともにすべるスキー
なんて楽しい！

Long and white snow course
We ski at sunrise
How fun!

Đường dài tuyết trắng tinh
Chúng em trượt tuyết lúc bình minh
Thật thú vị biết bao!

Huỳnh Ngọc Mai Khanh
Huynh Ngoc Mai Khanh
age14
Vietnam（ベトナム）

She has beautiful
Violet slippers with bows
Dancing to the mirror

Tal on Ilusad
Lillad lipsuga sussid
Tantsib peegli ees

Maibrit Tint
age 6
Estonia（エストニア）

あのこはきれいな
リボンのついたすみれいろのくつで
かがみのまえでおどる

Ribbon twirling high
Flying through the clear blue sky
Caught it just in time

Stephany Yeo Xyn-Ru
age 9
Singapore（シンガポール）

高く回るリボン
澄んだ青い空へ飛び
うまくつかまえた

When I cross the mountain on my skies
The pristine snow
Makes me dream

Quand je traverse la montagne sur mes skies
La neige immaculée
Me fait rêver

スキーで山越え
真っ白な雪で
夢ごこち

Guichet Maouche Emi
age10
France（フランス）

The ball rolls
Everbody in the stands
Freezed

El balón rueda
Todo el mundo en la grada
Muerto de frío

ボールが転がる
スタンドの人たちは
凍りつく

Rubén Marzo Aguirre
age11
Spain（スペイン）

Autumn wind
Take a leaf
Take a balls

Ovento de outono
Leva a folha
Leva a bola

秋風
木の葉を飛ばせ
ボールを転がせ

Cecília Maria Alcobia
age12
Portugal（ポルトガル）

72

雪のつもった松がじっと見てる
細いエッジが氷のもようを描く
あたたかいココアが待っている

Snowy pine trees watch
Thin blades craft icy patterns
Hot cocoa awaits

Sumayyah Deen
age11
Australia（オーストラリア）

Snowy pine trees watch
Thin blades craft icy patterns
Hot cocoa awaits

The wind is blowing past my ears
Skating in the park
The flowers smile happily

風在耳邊吹
我在公園滑排輪
花兒笑咪咪

郭 瀚天
Kuo Han-Tian
age 8
Taiwan（台湾／高雄）

耳のそばを風が吹き
公園でローラースケート
花たちもニコニコ笑顔

ЛЫЖНИК БЕСШУМНО
СКОЛЬЗИТ ПО ТРОПИНКАМ ЛЕСА
А ДЕРЕВЬЯ СМОТРЯТ

スキーヤーが音も立てずに
森の道に沿ってすべっていく
木々が見ている

Skier is silently
Gliding along the paths of the forest
And the trees are watching

Лыжник бесшумно
Скользит по тропинкам леса
А деревья смотрят

Малыгина Виктория
Malygina Viktoria
age12
Russia（ロシア）

水鳥たち
スケートでダンス
氷の上で

Rain birds
Are dancing with sled
On the ice

Yağmur kuşları
Kızakla dans ediyor
Buzun üstünde

Inci Duru Bayer
age13
Turkey（トルコ）

雪が降って
山々の頂上は
スキーの花ざかり

After snowfall
Tops of mountains
Burst into blooming skis

Sniegui prisnigus
Ant aukščiausių kalnelių
Pražysta slidės

Skaistė Kučinskaitė
Skaiste Kucinskaite
age12
Lithuania（リトアニア）

夜が明ける、出発だ
さわやかなあたたかい風が顔に
水を切って進む

Dawn breaks, I set off
A fresh, warm breeze on my face
Gliding through water

Hattie Corbishley
age11
UK（英国）

自然のなかをトレッキング
小川やぬかるみを渡って
ゆっくり休みたいな

Trekking in nature
Crossing streams and muddy tracks
Long for a good rest

Goh Zhou Rui
age10
Singapore（シンガポール）

青い海
青い波
魚と泳ぐサーファー

The blue sea
Blue waves
A surfer swims with fish

La mer bleue
Les vagues bleues
Un surfer nage avec les poissons

Fresnel Leeloo
age 8
France（フランス）

Racing back and forth
In the bright blue ocean's bay
Summer paddling

レースは抜きつ抜かれつ
輝く青い海の入り江
夏のパドリング

Sablan Laila
age10
USA（米国／グアム）

氷の上をすべる
上着の前は開けて
心も開いて

Skating over the ice
My jacket is open
And so is my heart

Uiskudega jääl
Jaki hõlmad lahtised
Nagu ka süda

Laura-Mia Neemla
age13
Estonia（エストニア）

雪の日
少年がスケートをしている
スケート靴をはかずに

Snowy day
A boy skating
Without the skates

Día nevado
Un niño patinando
Sin los patines

Lucía Arrabales Reillo
age13
Spain（スペイン）

公園をジョギング
咲いている花は
散るのが早い

Jogging in the park
Flowers in blossom, too quickly
Falling to the ground

Tan Xin Rou
age 9
Singapore（シンガポール）

Jogging in the park
flowers in blossom, so quickly
falling to the ground

ちっちゃなカタツムリ
なんて速（はや）いの
秋（あき）のかけっこならね

Little snail was
Also how fast
In fall race

Küçük salyongoz
Ne kadar da hızlıdır
Güz koşusunda

Başak Ünlü
Basak Unlu
age11
Turkey（トルコ）

第十六回「世界こどもハイクコンテスト」は「スポーツ」をテーマとして開催されました。これは、東京二〇二〇オリンピック開催に因んで設定されたテーマでしたが、ご存知の通り、新型コロナウイルスの感染拡大により、オリンピックは一年延期される運びとなりました。今回のハイクコンテスト自体も、新型コロナウイルスの影響を大きく受けました。世界各地で二〇一九年九月から開催されたコンテストは、二〇二〇年に入ってからの感染拡大により、学校が閉鎖されて作品の回収が困難になったり、せっかく集められた作品も審査会が実施できず審査が進まなかったり、と困難に直面しました。それでも、関係の皆さまのご尽力により、三十八の国と地域から二万を超える作品が集められ、一九九〇年の第一回から三十年にわたって寄せられた作品の累計数は、七十二万に達しました。

このコンテストの最大の特徴は、子どもたちが自国の言葉で綴った三行詩と自ら描いた絵で作品が構成されている点です。世界中から集まった作品を見ると、国や地域によってさかんなスポーツに違いがあるのが分かりますが、スポーツの楽しさやスポーツを通じて得た絆は万国共通のものであることが伝わってきます。また、そこには各国・各地域の気候、自然、文化、習慣の特色が垣間見られ、子どもたちの豊かな感性や多様な視点には目を見張るものがあります。

私たちは今、新型コロナウイルスという未知の敵からの挑戦を受け、国家間の往来や社会的な交流を制限しながらこれと戦っています。このような危機下においては、本来国境を越えて連携を深めるべきですが、どうしても自国や自分の社会を優先し、他者を批判する考えが台頭しがちです。そのような状況においても、日本で誕生した短い詩形「俳句」の文化を世界に発信し、そこから発展した「ハイク」の作品を通じて、子どもたちが互いに関心を持ち、理解し、認め合うきっかけを提供するという意味において、今回の「世界こどもハイクコンテスト」は、これまで以上に大きな意義があったのではないかと考えます。

なお、このコンテストの開催にあたり、国際俳句交流協会、国際交流基金、日本ユニセフ協会、各国大使館、外務省、在外公館、文化庁、ブロンズ新社、日本航空などの皆さまから多大なるご支援、ご協力を賜りました。この場をお借りして、心より御礼を申し上げます。

公益財団法人JAL財団
常務理事　池田　江津子

＊第十七回「世界こどもハイクコンテスト」は、二〇二二年に「まち」をテーマに開催する予定です。世界中の子どもたちからの作品をお待ちしています。詳細は、公益財団法人JAL財団のホームページ（http://www.jal-foundation.or.jp/）をご覧ください。

おわりに

Epilogue

The theme for the 16th World Children's Haiku Contest was "Sports." This theme was chosen as the Olympic Games Tokyo 2020 was to be held this year, but as you know, the Olympic Games have been postponed for one year due to the new coronavirus, or COVID-19. It also affected our contest this year. Worldwide regional contests which were held from September 2019 faced considerable difficulties from the spread of COVID-19 since the beginning of 2020, because it became difficult to collect haiku works due to school closures and haiku that were submitted could not be judged as selection meetings could not be held. Regardless, with considerable effort by the related parties, over 20,000 haiku were gathered from 38 countries and regions, bringing the total over the past 30 years since the start of the contest to 720,000.

The main feature of this contest is that the three-line poem written in the children's own language is attached with their drawing. The drawings show differences in the sport that is popular in their country or region and reveal that the enjoyment of playing sports and friendships built through sports is universal. Furthermore, they give us an idea of the features of the local climate, nature, culture, and customs, and the children's amazing sensitivity and diverse perspectives.

Today we are being challenged by and fighting an unknown virus while restricting travel between countries and social interactions. Under these circumstances, we should be deepening coordination across borders but instead tend to prioritize our own country and society and be critical of others. Therefore, we feel that this year's World Children's Haiku Contest was meaningful more than ever before in the sense that the introduction and composition of haiku, the world's shortest poem born in Japan, provided children an opportunity to strengthen their mutual interest and understanding and to accept each other even in the current situation.

The World Children's Haiku Contest was made possible with the great support and cooperation from the Haiku International Association, the Japan Foundation, the Japan Committee for UNICEF, embassies in countries concerned, the Ministry of Foreign Affairs of Japan, overseas diplomatic establishments, the Agency for Cultural Affairs, Bronze Publishing Inc., and Japan Airlines. We would like to express our sincere appreciation for their kind assistance.

Etsuko Ikeda
Managing Director
JAL Foundation

The 17th "World Children's Haiku Contest" will be held in 2021 under the theme of "Hometowns". We look forward to seeing haiku from children all over the world. For more details, please visit the JAL Foundation website. (http://www.jal-foundation.or.jp)

Балерина крутит фуэте...
Тихо стучат пуанты.
Вне театра-листопад.

アンゴラとラトビアのコンテストは開催されましたが、新型コロナウイルス等の事情により、コンテストの開催期間、および審査が大幅に遅れたため、本紙への掲載はできておりません。

Contests were held in Angola and Latvia due to coronavirus, circumstances, etc but the period of the contest and the judging process were significantly delayed, so the contest has not been published in this magazine.

INDEX

地球歳時記

スポーツのうた
Impressions of Sports

2021年3月25日　初版第1刷発行

編　者　公益財団法人JAL財団

装　丁　籾山真之(snug.)
編　集　籾山伸子(snug.)
発行者　若月眞知子
発行所　ブロンズ新社
　　　　東京都渋谷区神宮前6-31-15-3B
　　　　03-3498-3272
　　　　https://www.bronze.co.jp/

印　刷　吉原印刷
製　本　難波製本